Special thanks from the family to Grandma,
who makes so much possible.
— The Fogarty Family

First Edition June 2021

ISBN 978-1-7371089-0-0 : Ingram Sparks paperback

ISBN 978-1-7371089-1-7 : KDP Kids paperback

ISBN 978-1-7371089-2-4 : Ingram Sparks hardback

ISBN 978-1-7371089-3-1 : KDP Kids ebook

ISBN 978-1-7371089-4-8 : Ingram Sparks ebook

Julianne and the Shaggy Dog

Written by James Fogarty

Illustrated by Mai S. Kemble

At the end of a street that was shaded by trees,
Lived a sweet little girl with two knobby, scraped knees.

Her house was quite tall, the corners not square;
Bird chirps and bug calls swam through the air.

The backyard was spacious and covered with flowers,
Where this little girl spent most of her hours.

A winding stone path that went to and fro,
Ending up in the woods, and away she would go.

One day she made plans for quite a new venture,
The sun was up high, and she wanted adventure.

Prepared with supplies she had slung on her back,
She kissed parents goodbye and ran down the track.

This path wandered by a few creeks and a brook,
Past ant hills and bird's nests where she stopped for a look.

Then across a green field where the path took a bend
Sat a great shaggy dog. Could he be a new friend?
She paused and she pondered; the dog did the same.
Then slowly and calmly towards her he came.

She tossed off her backpack and waited a bit.
When he plopped down beside her, she decided to sit.
She scratched the old dog, his grizzled old maw,
His shaggy black coat, his white fleckled paw.

He nuzzled her hand as the sun neared its peak,
Looked deep in her eyes and started to speak.
"I've lost my green ball somewhere deep in the trees.
I'm not able to get it. Could you help me please?"

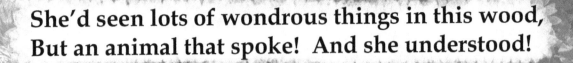

She'd seen lots of wondrous things in this wood,
But an animal that spoke! And she understood!

She scratched 'hind his ears and nodded assent.
He trotted beside her and together they went.

Out of the field and into the green,
They arrived at the tallest tree ever seen.

The branches were thick, spiraling up to the top.
At the base of this tree the dog came to a stop.

"A large bird has nabbed it and flown away high;
The ball's in its nest now, up there in the sky."

"Shall I climb up to get it?" she asked with a frown,
"If it's very far up, then it's very far down."

The dog didn't speak, but she knew what he meant,
and with a big leap, she began her ascent.

The first limb was easy, but then it got harder;
The safe looking ground got farther and farther.

She soon heard a sound that filled her with dread,
Right there was a beehive, just over her head!

Her skin prickled up, she felt chills on her arm,
The bees were now buzzing, but she meant them no harm.

She took a deep breath, then suddenly froze.
Cross-eyed she saw a bee right on her nose!

It waddled and prodded and looked straight in her eyes;
She froze and she shivered but held in her cries.

It stayed just a moment then flew back in the air.
She sighed with relief and clambered from there.

She was perilously high, the sky nearing too,
Right there! - was the nest; she knew just what to do.

She leaned on her foot and her shaky left leg;
Saw the ball in the nest, wrapped up like an egg.

She reached out to grab the shaggy dog's ball,
When the bird swooped right in, and she started to fall.

She grabbed at a branch which rattled the nest,
Made it slip to one side; gravity did the rest.

The ball fell away, bounced left and bounced right
And fell out of the tree and out of her sight.

The bird fussed about, put its home back in order,
While the girl quickly turned to a branch that could hold her.

Back down the tree, avoiding the bees,
She hopped to the ground and fell to her knees.

The dog looked expectant, but said not a word.
She said, "I'm sorry. I was surprised by the bird."

He nodded and sighed, she rubbed his black ear.
"We should go looking; it has to be near."

"It fell from the branches, hopped a stone in the brook,
It bounched over there so that's where we should look."

"If I were a ball, which way would I go?
Well...I doubt very much as a ball I would know."

But she realized a ball would always roll down
So they followed its path down the slope of the ground.

There at the base of the hill they stood on
Sat the ball on some stones it had nestled upon.

But as she reached for the ball, she started to wonder
Why the earth was now trembling and rolling like thunder...

They heard a loud roar- searching fast left and right -
They saw a large bear, what a terrible sight!

They tried running back, but the girl slipped and stumbled
The bear thundered on and she felt the ground rumble.

It seemed like this must be a terrible end
From sharp teeth and long claws with points that could rend.

The bear came toward her; he wanted that ball!
Then she heard racing toward her the best sound of them all.

A rush of wind, a dark blurry shape
And suddenly the dog had the bear by the nape.

The dog clung on tight as the bear started to rear,
And she knew now for sure she had nothing to fear.

She reached for a branch, way up on her toes,
Broke it, turned back, and swung for its nose.

The sharp pokey branch swished through the air,
It was two against one now; that didn't seem fair!

The bear fell back down, facing dog and fierce girl,
Its courage was failing, its head in a whirl.

A few more loud snarls, some more swings with the stick.
The bear turned and ran - that did the trick!

They jumped and hoorayed, they both felt so grand,
With one final reach she had the ball in her hand!
She tossed it into her bag to climb up the rocks,
When she came face to face with a sly looking fox.

He was a soft looking creature, burnt orange and brown,
He stepped lightly toward her, padding soft on the ground.

He deftly stepped closer with a delicate walk,
And with a silk sounding voice he started to talk.

"What's in the bag? What is it you hid?
You cannot deceive me, I saw what you did."

She said, "I'm not hiding anything; this dog lost his ball.
I'm helping return it, that's it and that's all."

"Then it must be you've found the ball that I own.
I lost it, back there, when I'd overthrown."
He eyed the bag greedily, his tail gave a twitch.
She looked back and forth suddenly not knowing which.

There was something here she could not define,
This fox didn't seem like the ball throwing kind.

He seemed a bit edgy, he was licking his tooth,
She decided to find if he was telling the truth.

What could she think of to help her decide?
To tell if he'd been honest or if he had lied?

"So if it's your ball, as you say that it is...
What color is it? Answer that quiz."

He waited to answer till it was long overdue
Then more certain than not, he simply said, "Blue."

The answer he gave made her deeply relieved.
She saw that the fox could not be believed.

She held out her bag, inside out, to be seen.
Deep inside was the ball, entirely green.

"I'm sorry, Sir Fox, that's entirely wrong.
It can't be your ball, so please move along."

The fox held her gaze, then he glanced at the dog,
As he turned and he left, with a slow, lazy jog.

She grinned at the dog and gave his ball back.
He turned and he dropped it right into her pack.

"Hold on to it for me, and whenever you could,
Come throw it for me out here in the wood."

She had an idea- "Hey, what do you say
You come back to my house- it could be every day!"

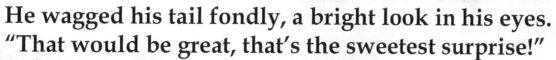

He wagged his tail fondly, a bright look in his eyes.
"That would be great, that's the sweetest surprise!"

She wrapped up the dog in a loving embrace.
He loved her right back, licking her face.

"I'm so happy you'll come," she said with a smile,
"But let's head on home, we've been here a while."

She cinched up her bag then strapped on the same,
And followed the path heading home as she came.

With new life in their steps, they bounded away,
And got bảçk to their home by the end of the day.

The End